Listening *at*
Golgotha

Listening *at* Golgotha

JESUS' WORDS FROM THE CROSS

PETER STOREY

Art by Jan L. Richardson

UPPER
ROOM BOOKS®
NASHVILLE

Cover and interior design: GoreStudio, Inc.
Cover and interior art: Jan L. Richardson
First Printing: 2004

    LIBRARY OF CONGRESS CATALOGING-IN-PUBLICATION DATA
Storey, Peter John, 1938–
   Listening at Golgotha : Jesus' words from the cross / by Peter
Storey; art by Jan L. Richardson.
        p. cm.
   Includes bibliographical references.
   ISBN 0-8358-9884-9
   1. Jesus Christ–Seven last words–Meditations. 2. Holy Week–
Prayer-books and devotions–English. I. Title
BT456.S68 2004
238.96'35–dc22   2004011372

To

JOHN, CHRISTOPHER,
DAVID, AND ALAN

*Thank you for
the joy your lives bring us
and the different gifts
you share in God's world.*

Contents

Introduction   9

THE FIRST WORD   15
"Father, forgive them; for they do not
know what they are doing."

THE SECOND WORD   27
"Today you will be with me in Paradise."

THE THIRD WORD   39
"Woman, here is your son. . . . Here is
your mother."

THE FOURTH WORD   49
"My God, my God, why have
you forsaken me?"

THE FIFTH WORD   61
"I am thirsty."

THE SIXTH AND SEVENTH WORDS   73
"It is finished."
"Father, into your hands I commend
my spirit."

THE FIRST DAY OF THE WEEK   83

Notes 89

About the Author 91

About the Artist 93

Introduction

$\mathcal{E}$VERY GOOD FRIDAY, all around the world, in tiny chapels and soaring cathedrals, the disciples of Jesus Christ gather to watch with him from noon to three o'clock—the final three hours of his crucifixion when darkness covered the earth. During the three-hour vigil, we listen again for his seven utterances from the cross.

The words of a dying person are always significant but never more so than when that person is Jesus, Son of God. The Seven Words have come to be invested with profound meaning for the church. They can be saving words for us as individuals also.

I preached these meditations on the Seven Words in Duke University Chapel during Holy Week of 2002. I am deeply grateful to then Dean of the Chapel, Dr. William Willimon, for that opportunity to proclaim Christ's Passion. This book is immensely enhanced by Jan Richardson's remarkable illustrations—each one a meditation in itself—and I am thankful for her artistic insight into Christ's Passion.

These thoughts were born during nearly four decades of ministry in South Africa, where the church had to learn a Cross-shaped ministry under the shadow of apartheid's oppression. Across South Africa's cruel political landscape of that period, Holy Week was always a strengthening time for the hurting victims of apartheid. The poor and oppressed and the people of faith trying to offer resistance seemed to know instinctively that in this pain-drenched narrative, their own struggles would be embraced and given meaning by the sorrow of God.

Not surprisingly, it was those most sinned against in our society who seemed most able to grasp the self-giving mystery of atonement. The issue of whether one would die rather than kill to overcome evil was at that time an existential dilemma demanding painful choice each day. Since the Son of God, faced by implacable evil, determined that he would be willing to die for the world but would never kill for it, Holy Week and Good Friday in particular presented an inescapable challenge to us all.

That challenge is only one of many layers of meaning that flow from the Cross of Jesus. All of us need to enter into our own conversation with that Cross and the one who hangs upon it. If we believe that "Christ died for our sins in accordance with the scriptures" (1 Corinthians 15.3), we each need to bring to Calvary the issues of sin and righteousness, both personal and systemic, that we wrestle with in our time and place. We need to do this with utmost seriousness if the Easter that follows Good Friday is to mean anything to us at all. We cannot live in the power of the Resurrection unless we have walked with Jesus to Calvary and paused to look and listen there. We need to make space for the vulnerability, pain, and self-offering of the Crucifixion to engage us deeply, bringing us to an awed penitence. Only out of such penitence can transformation and new life be born.

For centuries the words Jesus spoke *from* the cross have helped Christians to hear more clearly the saving word God spoke *through* the Cross. If these brief meditations serve that purpose, I am content.

How to Use This Book

Readers might begin with the first word on Palm Sunday, meditating on one word each day. Spend time contemplating both the illustration and the text. Allow God to speak to you through the questions—or the silence—evoked by each word and make the closing prayer your own.

Following this schedule will bring you to the last two words on Good Friday. Holy Saturday could be used to return and meditate on all Seven Words. Then on Easter Day read "The First Day of the Week."

Peter Storey

THE FIRST
WORD

"Father, forgive them;
for they do not know what
they are doing."

LUKE 23:34

Two others also, who were criminals, were led away to be put to death with him. When they came to the place that is called The Skull, they crucified Jesus there with the criminals, one on his right and one on his left. Then Jesus said, "Father, forgive them; for they do not know what they are doing."

—Luke 23:32–34

We know what they were doing! They were busy with things only too familiar to our world: the greed that sells a friend for money; the fear that denies one's leader for survival; the cynicism that smears an innocent for political gain; the cruelty that tortures a prisoner for entertainment; the expediency that washes its hands of moral decision making; the mob spirit that exults in a victim's suffering; the stupidity that calls good evil and evil good. That's what they were doing. If they didn't know it, we do. We know about this stuff.

More important is what Jesus was doing.

Jesus was about to die, and he would die as he had lived. A special wholeness of being happens when a person's thoughts, words, and deeds all come together to tell the same story. That sort of congruence is what we call integrity. For most of us, no matter how ardently we seek it, total integrity eludes us. Our deeds too often fall short of our declared intentions; many of our words bear no resemblance to what we are really thinking at the time; and some of our thoughts must simply remain veiled in shame.

Jesus was different. Jesus taught as he believed, lived as he taught, and died as he lived. His life was one of seamless integrity. When his hands were pinned excruciatingly to the wood and he cried, "Forgive them, Father!" Jesus was living out in his dying one the hardest of his own teachings:

> Love your enemies and pray for those
> who persecute you, so that you
> may be children of your Father in
> heaven. (Matthew 5:44–45)

Many find Jesus' teaching on enemy love and forgiveness a stumbling block to faith. Because we find it too difficult to practice, we dismiss it as unrealistic and utopian.

We should think again, and we should pray that it is not unrealistic, because this congruence of Jesus—the consistency between his teaching on forgiveness and his action on the cross—is really our only hope. It is all that stands between us and the consequences of our monumental frailty. Thank God today that Jesus died as he lived, because with those words, "Father, forgive . . . ," he forgives us all, and he forgives us still.

Even so, as we marvel at this way of forgiveness, the enemy love of Jesus seems beyond the reach of ordinary mortals. Yet, if Jesus' mission is to be fulfilled, and if the world is to be any different because of him, this same spirit must find ways to penetrate our resistant lives.

The Orthodox churches have an ancient story about Good Friday that speaks of this need. It tells of the blood of Jesus running down the cross and soaking into the ground, penetrating to the depths of the earth, until, finally, it reaches the bones of Adam and Eve, healing them where they lie in shame. When we allow Calvary's forgiving stream to permeate all the way to the primal places of our failure, it heals us even there. It makes the difference in otherwise defeated lives. Ordinary people, touched by the power of the Cross, can become extraordinary in their capacity to love and forgive.

Remember Stephen, the first Christian martyr. At the end of his trial, he looked up to heaven and said, "Look, I see the heavens opened and the Son of Man standing at the right hand of God!" People then set about stoning him to death. As he fell to his knees under this onslaught, his dying words were, "Lord, do not hold this sin against them" (Acts 7:55–60). Stephen had received the gift of enemy love, the power to forgive.

Another young man stood watch as those executioners went about their business. He was named Saul, and his transformation began that day. Some time later, he too would be touched by this life-shattering experience called forgiveness.

Struck helpless and blind, he would be at the mercy of the very people he had come to kill in Damascus. Then, one of them named Ananias would come right into Saul's lodging, greet him with the word "Brother," and restore his sight. And Saul would become love's prisoner (Acts 9:1–19).

With those words, "Father, forgive them," a new way of life patterned by Jesus has been passed on from Calvary to us all. Difficult though it may be, the practice of enemy love lies at the center of our salvation story. Too many Christians fail the gospel at this crucial point, but its challenge will not go away, and in each generation God still gives us glimpses of the Christ power of forgiving love.

Remember when Martin Luther King Jr. and his followers in the civil rights movement staked their lives on the power of enemy love? Because of Jesus, King knew there was something more important than defeating people. He believed that forgiving love had the capacity to change them instead. And the amazing thing is that not only did he seem to live this way, but thousands of ordinary people believed him and did so too. They braved beatings, death threats, prison, and worse, all the while holding on to King's example of refusing to hate those they were up against.

In South Africa the millions of black people who suffered horrific indignities under the awful policy of apartheid have made forgiving their enemies the key to rebuilding their nation. They have put aside their primitive right to revenge and embraced something more costly yet much more hopeful. Over twenty thousand cases of torture, assassination, maiming, and other gross human rights violations were heard by South Africa's Truth and Reconciliation Commission, and some seven thousand perpetrators of these abuses appeared to ask for forgiveness. Not a single case of private retribution has been recorded. Here is a nation trusting in the spirit of pardon and reconciliation.

And so must we. If we claim to follow Jesus, we must believe that love, not force, is God's mightiest weapon; that evil may seem to be rampant as it certainly appeared to be on Good Friday, but it is only the second strongest power in the universe.

Let us pray for grace to live by these words from the cross:

Father, forgive them; for they do not know what they are doing.

FOR REFLECTION

Where am I hearing this word about forgiveness spoken today? Where does this word most need to be spoken in my world, my life? Whom and what am I being called to forgive—really forgive?

Prayer

Holy Jesus, your forgiving love saves
    and disturbs me.
Without it, I am lost,
Yet, if I receive it, I must practice it.
By your mercy, make me merciful;
By your forgiveness, help me to forgive
    as I have been forgiven.
Amen.

THE SECOND
WORD

---

*"Today you
will be with me
in Paradise."*

LUKE 23:43

One of the criminals who were hanged there kept deriding him and saying, "Are you not the Messiah? Save yourself and us!" But the other rebuked him, saying, "Do you not fear God, since you are under the same sentence of condemnation? And we indeed have been condemned justly, for we are getting what we deserve for our deeds, but this man has done nothing wrong." Then he said, "Jesus, remember me when you come into your kingdom." He replied, "Truly I tell you, today you will be with me in Paradise."

—LUKE 23:39–43

*B*ecause he died as he lived, Jesus did not die entirely alone. His life had always been one of solidarity and identification with the least and lowest. This man who had begun life as a refugee, who had known poverty and hunger, labor and sorrow, had spent his time with the common people and those who lived on the margins. We should not be surprised, then, that on the day of his dying, Jesus was once more in the company of those whom society had cast out.

The book of Hebrews tells us that to "sanctify the people by his own blood," Jesus "also suffered outside the city gate," like the animals used in sacrifice. It calls us to go to him "outside the camp and bear the abuse he endured" (Hebrews 13:12–13). The New English Bible uses the word *stigma*. It seems that if we want to come near to this Christ, we must follow him in being among those whom we would not always want to associate with.

Some tell us that following Jesus is a simple matter of inviting him into our hearts. But when we do that, Jesus always asks, "May I bring my friends?" And when we look at them, we see that they are not the kind of company we like to keep. The friends of Jesus are the outcasts, the marginalized, the poor, the homeless, the rejected—the lepers of life.

We hesitate and ask, "Jesus, must we really have them too?"

Jesus replies, "Love me, love my friends!"

THESE MEN HANGING on each side of Jesus were criminals. They were thieves or rebels, condemned to this barbarous death because that is what the law required. The law of crime and punishment will always be a blunt instrument, but we decent people don't ask too many questions. We rely on the law to guard our lives and our possessions; it keeps the barbarians at bay. Conventional wisdom would conclude that the felons on each side of Jesus got what they deserved because they had fallen below the standards of decent society.

The third person—in the middle—was different. He was being executed not for falling below society's standards but for rising above them. Jesus was going to die not for being bad but for being too good.

We should not be surprised by this reversal. The law can be used as often to oppress as to protect, and our world resents those who challenge its venality, its accommodation with moral mediocrity. When George Bernard Shaw learned of the assassination of Mahatma Gandhi, his cryptic comment was, "It shows how dangerous it is to be too good."[1]

From his first chapter, the author of John's Gospel declares the world's rejection of Jesus' radical goodness. Jesus is the "true light, which enlightens everyone," coming into a world of darkness, and John says that "he came to what was his own, and his own people did not accept him" (John 1:9, 11). Later he warns that there are those who prefer darkness to light because their deeds are evil. "For all who do evil hate the light and do not come to the light, so that their deeds may not be exposed" (John 3:19–20). At one point, Jesus speaks bluntly to those who oppose him: "Now you are trying to kill me, a man who has told you the truth that I heard from God" (John 8:40).

It is just as well that we stand for a while beneath Jesus' cross and ponder the consequences of radical goodness. We should know what it costs before we decide to follow this man; we should recognize how dangerous it is to be good.

THE MEN WHO hung on the three crosses also turned them into very different instruments upon which to die.

One was a cross of *rebellion*. The felon there wasted no time on introspection, spending his last hours hurling his anger onto everyone around, including Jesus. Sadly, it blinded him to the hope right beside him and blocked entrance to what Jesus would have gladly given.

Anger can do the same in our lives. It is corrosive and destructive. Our anger against life blocks the flow of grace with great lumps of resentment. We need to pray that the noises in our heads—our resentments, angers, hurts, and hatreds—do not close our hearts to Christ's mercy. Desmond Tutu says, "God . . . has such a deep reverence for our freedom that [God] would much rather see us go freely to hell than compel us to go to heaven."[2] Do not let your anger prevent you from discovering that the words "Father, forgive . . ." include you.

The second cross was one of *repentance*. For the second man, something important and life-changing dawned. This Jesus was indeed different. Not only was he innocent of any crime, but there was more: this Nazarene's response, the forgiving cry that burst from his lips as the nails were hammered home, stirred a spirit of contrition in this other soul. He cried, "Jesus, remember me."

In that moment, he became the first for whom the central cross, the cross of Jesus, became the Cross of *redemption*.

For us to be made right with God, repentance is always necessary, but repentance is not so much a condition for forgiveness as a consequence of it. We human beings often hold back our forgiveness for some slight or hurt until we at least see signs of contrition. Not so with God: on the cross, the word of forgiveness is spoken first; it gives birth to one felon's contrite cry. This truth changes the equation of salvation. When will we learn that we do not repent in order to find pardon? We repent because we discover how deeply we have been pardoned—how much we have been forgiven.

Jesus responds to our slightest sign of contrition. Is it possible to speak of joy in the heart of Jesus on the cross? In one sense, yes, because surely this interchange with the contrite criminal represents the essence of Jesus' reason for coming.

I can imagine bystanders listening to this man in his desperate need, crying, "Jesus, remember me when you come into your kingdom!" Perhaps some recalled a story told on a Galilean hill, a story that explored the geography of their souls, about a father and his son, a family home, and a far country. When the son had effectively wrecked his life, this headstrong, selfish boy dragged himself home with hope of nothing more than a meal and a bed. But at the first sight of him on the horizon, his father ran to meet him, fell on his neck, and kissed him. "Put a ring on his finger and sandals on his feet. . . . for this son of mine was dead and is alive again; he was lost and is found" (Luke 15:11–24).

> Truly I tell you, today you will be with me in Paradise.

Today! The early Methodist circuit riders of the American frontier never tired of telling their hearers that the offer of Christ's forgiveness and salvation was available now—immediately! There was no need to wait.

We come to the Cross to make that discovery again and to cry, "Remember me, Jesus!" Today!

For Reflection

Where, in today's world, does this word
of extravagant hospitality and mercy need
most desperately to be heard? What
changes in my living and loving are
evoked by this word? How would Jesus
want me to demonstrate this word?

Prayer

Holy Jesus, love held you to the cross for
    my sake, but not mine alone.
Your love is frightening in its breadth
    and depth;
When I embrace it, it stretches my
    poor spirit.
Enlarge my heart to make space for
    your friends;
Let me love as one forgiven.
Today.
Amen.

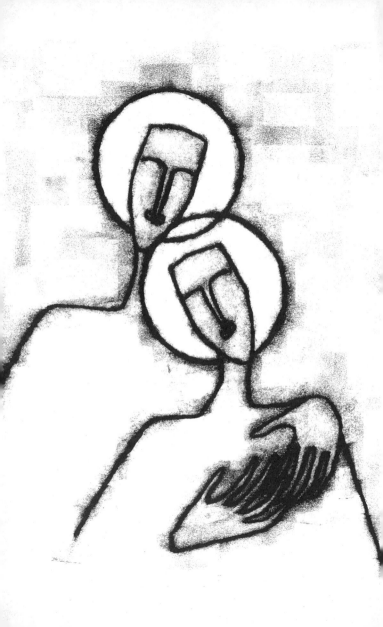

THE THIRD
WORD

---

*"Woman,
here is your son.... Here
is your mother."*

JOHN 19:26

Meanwhile, standing near the cross of Jesus were his mother, and his mother's sister, Mary the wife of Clopas, and Mary Magdalene. When Jesus saw his mother and the disciple whom he loved standing beside her, he said to his mother, "Woman, here is your son." Then he said to the disciple, "Here is your mother." And from that hour the disciple took her into his own home.

—John 19:25–27

Standing below Jesus' cross is the woman who gave him birth, who nursed him at her breast, who nurtured him in childhood and youth. Now the sword promised by Simeon when her baby was presented at the Temple has come to pierce her heart.

Just three decades after his birth, her flesh and blood and bone—her son—hangs in front of her.

Mary had often struggled with who this son really was. We don't know when the first stirrings of divinity welled up in his humanness, but at a mere twelve years of age he already had been lost to the family for three long days, to be found in the Temple precincts, debating its learned men. Even then there was a depth in Jesus that she could not fully reach.

John tells us that Mary and Jesus' brothers were with him in his early ministry. Mary played a major part in the first of his great signs in Cana of Galilee, urging Jesus to come to the aid of an embarrassed young couple by rescuing their wedding party (John 2:1–12).

But then came another day when Jesus had to remind his mother and brothers that he now had a much wider family:

"Who are my mother and my brothers?" And looking at those who sat around him, he said, "Here are my mother and my brothers! Whoever does the will of God is my brother and sister and mother." (Mark 3:31–35)

This passage might come as a shock to those of us who put a high premium on close family life, but we shall see that these apparently harsh words are actually the hope of a new world. This would become evident later, but meanwhile, Mary had kept all these things in her heart—the things she understood and those she didn't. Mothers can do that. She had known from the beginning that this Jesus–child was only loaned to her.

Now he is dying, and amazingly, even in this agony, the needs of others still touch Jesus more intensely than his own. We do not know Mary's family circumstances at this time, but we know enough about the vulnerability of older women in those days to be fearful for her.

Once, outside a village called Nain, Jesus and his disciples had come upon a little funeral procession where a widowed mother was burying her only son. The custom of the day was not kind to women without any male support; in addition to the grief of loss, this woman would suffer cruel marginalization in her village. Deeply moved by her brokenness, Jesus had raised that young man from death and returned him to his mother. The procession of death had become a joyous celebration of life.

Now, from the cross, Jesus honors the fifth commandment. He must ensure his mother's safekeeping too. He looks at her and at the disciple who stands with her and makes arrangements for her care. "There is your son . . . there is your mother."

This is Jesus' last will and testament to his mother. He has owned nothing but the clothes on his back, and the soldiers have diced for those. But he does bequeath her a new son. To John the disciple he gives a new mother.

Here we see the beginning of something profoundly different for all followers of Jesus everywhere and in every age. This poignant interchange on Good Friday is a marker for a revolution in our under-standing of *community*. Jesus entrusts the life and welfare of another to one of his fol-lowers, and he places upon that new rela-tionship the value we reserve for our closest family unit.

No longer will the obligation of mutual care depend upon blood relationship, but all will be welcomed as the one family of Christ. No more will our first loyalty be to tribe or nation or clan. For Christians, "whoever does the will of God" will be our mothers, our sisters, our brothers, our fathers. From now on, the followers of Jesus will receive one another as gift, to be welcomed, honored, and cherished simply because Jesus has given them to us. That should be the only reason we need. "From that hour the disciple took her into his own home" (John 19:27).

When we take too much pride in "family churches," where neat, nuclear families dominate, we risk forgetting what Jesus did on Good Friday. "Family churches," for all their honoring of family life, may limit the much wider embrace of God's grace. Some priorities valued in family churches can be hostile to individuals who do not fit middle-class paradigms. They can exclude people Jesus would want to welcome. The world consists of many persons who have had to take different and often painful roads. The true community Jesus seeks makes space for them all.

From his cross, Jesus created a community that was to *become family* to the widow, the orphan, the outcast, and the stranger. Only when we have learned to offer welcome to the modern equivalent of people such as these do we come close to Christ's intention. It is not "family churches" but *"church families"* that the world needs.

I wonder if anyone watching at Calvary that day guessed that a new community, with the widest embrace in all the world, was being born. In this third word from the cross, we, as disciples of Jesus, are invited to accept a sacred trust. If we accept, can anybody suffer hunger, homelessness, or need? Would there be any lonely old people? Could there be a single unwanted child? If Jesus has made everyone kin to me, would that not make every war in history a civil war and every casualty a death in my family?

From the cross where he is nailed, *Jesus nails us to each other.* In doing so, he is giving birth to a new community.

FOR REFLECTION

What needs to change so that my life and my home church demonstrate this word of true community more clearly?

Prayer

Holy Jesus, I give thanks for your mother
    and all like her
who have borne the pain of loving
    too deeply.
Thank you for your gift the church.
Help me to receive as your gift all whom
    I encounter, whoever they are,
and to become family to them in your name.
Amen.

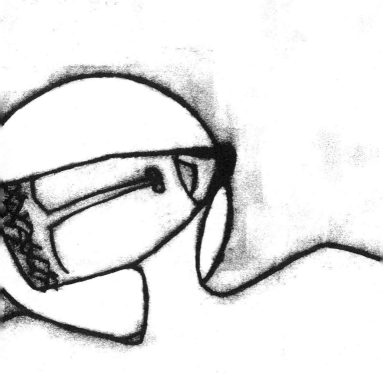

THE FOURTH
WORD

---

*"My God, my God,
why have you forsaken me?"*

MATTHEW 27:46

From noon on, darkness came over
the whole land until three in the
afternoon. And about three o'clock
Jesus cried with a loud voice, "Eli, Eli,
lema sabachthani?" that is, "My God,
my God, why have you forsaken me?"

—Matthew 27:45–46

*N*o sentence in scripture is more
clouded in horror and mystery than this cry
of dereliction.

Here the pain of the world's sin hurts
more than nails in flesh. Here is suffering
deeper than any seen before or since. Here
is the depth of the abyss. Here is desolation
so terrible that heaven itself draws a veil
over the scene.

> Darkness came over the whole
> land until three in the afternoon.
> (Matthew 27:45)

Humankind's greatest crime is under way. In our language, the word that expresses the deepest measure of agony is *excruciating*. It comes from the Latin *ex crucis*, or "from the cross." The word derives from this moment.

We need to tread reverently here because all our assumptions about Jesus are informed by hindsight, habit, and creed and viewed in the after light of an Easter that was yet to happen. Those assumptions can inure us to Jesus' dark night of the soul. But this cry tears all that away; it exposes Jesus' heart. This is a cry of abandonment and utter desolation; it is the cry of a deserted child of God. No one has ever been this much alone.

Could it be that in this moment, Jesus fears he has been abandoned in failure?

After three years of utter self-giving, of pouring out his heart, what has he to show? Is Jesus in that deep loneliness of wondering whether he has lived his life in vain? *Could I have been wrong? I trusted the Father—yet now it is so dark.*

OF COURSE, THIS loneliness is not entirely unfamiliar. Solitariness marks all of Jesus' life and ministry. In his humanity, even as a child, he thought and acted in ways that set him apart. What twelve-year-old would we expect to find his way into the inner sanctum of the Temple to talk with priests about God? What twelve-year-old would tell his parents he must be about *another* Father's business?

During his desert wanderings, Jesus was tossed about by temptations much deeper than any of us will know, temptations that can come only to one uniquely endowed with power from above. Only angels could minister to him then. Who else on this earth could counsel him about being the Lamb of God?

Can we imagine Jesus' many moments of near despair, when not only his detractors but those who called him Master utterly misunderstood his teaching? What can be lonelier than wanting to share God's deepest wisdom only to have your teaching constantly trivialized by cleverness; to carry with you the gift of eternal life and have it so often mistaken for something shallow and cheap?

The months leading up to this moment on the cross, when Jesus was the center of a seething vortex of conspiracy, were loneliest of all. He knew others were plotting his end; yet if he did not press on to Jerusalem, he would deny his identity.

That is loneliness, loneliness not of choice but of *vocation*. This Jesus, whose heart has been big enough for every beggar, every ruffian, every outcast he meets, is slowly abandoned by those who once thronged him. The Gospel writer tells us that "many of his disciples withdrew and no longer went about with him," so there is understandable pathos in his plea to the Twelve, "Do you also want to leave me?" (John 6:66–67, NEB).

Among Gethsemane's olive trees, as with doomed steps he goes where friends cannot follow, the loneliness of this prophet deepens:

> He said to his disciples, "Sit here while I go over there and pray." He took with him Peter and the two sons of Zebedee, and began to be grieved and agitated. Then he said to them, "I am deeply grieved, even to death; remain here, and stay awake with me." And going a little farther, he threw himself on the ground and prayed, "My Father, if it is possible,

let this cup pass from me; yet not
what I want but what you want."
(Matthew 26:36-39)

His fate is always to go on "a little far-ther." In the end, he knows he must go alone; that is the loneliness of vocation.

BUT WE TOO must go farther. With fear and trembling, we will ask, "Can there be more?" and the answer is, "Yes, there is more." Jesus' cry of dereliction from the cross carries an even deeper agony, and we can only touch the fringes of it.

The loneliness of vocation clearly took Jesus to places where his disciples could not follow spiritually—and ultimately, physically. But his intimate relationship with the Father remained unbroken, even in Gethsemane. Now, in the darkness of Calvary, *it is this relationship itself that is under assault*

If we have learned anything at all about sin, it is that sin separates. Jesus on the cross wrestles with the sinfulness of all the world; on the cross, he takes into himself all the weight of human wrong, all this world's brokenness, its darkness, its shame.

The apostle Paul goes as far into this agony as any of us should dare when he says the terrible words: "For our sake he made him to be sin who knew no sin" (2 Corinthians 5:21).

As Jesus absorbs all this weight of sin, is the Son's crucial sense of oneness with the Father severed? Is heaven's darkness the sign of a Father who can no longer bear to watch this deadly clash in his beloved's soul? We cannot know. None of us has known such a friendship with God; none can therefore know what this loneliness—this terrifying sense of absence—meant. "My God, my God, why have you forsaken me?"

But we all do know the sense of isolation that comes over *us* when we let wrongdoing invade our own lives. We know how we feel when we distance ourselves from full communion with our fellow humans and our God. We know the dis-ease within us until the wrong is repented and put right. We know that our sin makes us lonely, because deep inside us we know that we are made for friendship with God.

How desolate, how utterly abandoned, must Jesus have felt, carrying in his breaking heart not just your sin and mine but the sins of the whole world?

A darkness falls over the whole land. Jesus has gone where we cannot follow. All we can do is worship and wonder and wait while he does this work. For us.

FOR REFLECTION

Be silent.

Prayer

Holy Jesus, there was no suffering like
yours.
I am silent in the darkness,
Your darkness.
There can be no words,
Only worship.
Amen.

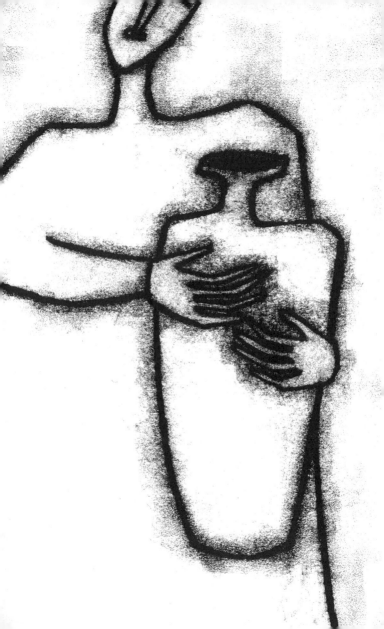

THE FIFTH
WORD

"I am thirsty."

JOHN 19:28

After this, when Jesus knew that all
was now finished, he said (in order to
fulfill the scripture), "I am thirsty." A jar
full of sour wine was standing there.
So they put a sponge full of the wine
on a branch of hyssop and held it to
his mouth.

—JOHN 19:28–29

Sometime during those dreadful six
hours, when dislocated joints and stretched
tendons can no longer keep his rib cage
open, and each breath is agony, Jesus
speaks those profoundly human words: "I
am thirsty." By now Jesus has become what
the prophet Isaiah described:

> His form, disfigured, has lost all the
>   likeness of a man,
> his beauty has changed beyond
>   human semblance. . . .
> tormented and humbled by suffering;
> . . . we held him of no account,
> a thing from which [all] turn away
>   their eyes. (Isaiah 53:2–3, NEB)

Now this broken thing speaks: "I am thirsty," and his executioners grant a final mercy, a dampened sponge on a branch of hyssop, touched to his cracked lips.

IF ANY SHOULD doubt the humanity of Jesus, here is proof of it.

When Jesus cries, "I am thirsty," he binds himself to the hurting of every generation and the sufferers of every century. The cry of thirst is the first sound of a newborn baby and the first plea of every mother after childbirth. Cries for water resound on every battlefield when the butchery is over. A moistened cloth to the lips is the last ministry we can offer a dying loved one. To thirst is to be one of us, and in the very human life of Jesus, the God of all the universe knew thirst.

The crucifixion of Jesus began long before he was born. It began in eternity, with a decision in the heart of God to journey from glory into poverty, from power to vulnerability, from all to nothing. The God of all the universe made a conscious decision to journey downward, to be born as a human baby in a finite world.

The apostle Paul marvels at this journey of Jesus:

> who, though he was in the form of God,
>   did not regard equality with God
>   as something to be exploited,
> but emptied himself,
>   taking the form of a slave.
> (Philippians 2:6–7)

That was the first step to Calvary, what theologians call the *kenosis*, self-emptying, of God. Calvary begins with the willing and loving release of divine power, the free decision to embrace our humanness.

But this?

Is it not enough to become one of us? Must Jesus also become victim to our worst brutalities? The apostle goes on:

> And being found in human form,
> he humbled himself
> and became obedient to the point
> of death—
> even death on a cross.
>
> (Philippians 2:7–8)

As Jesus cried out in thirst, maybe some out there in the crowd recalled that it hadn't always been like this. Perhaps a young couple, family friends, recall their wedding day just three years before, when the wine ran dry. The laughing young carpenter from Nazareth saved them from embarrassment by miraculously refilling the vats with the best wine of all. None had gone thirsty that day. Now he is dying, pleading desperately for a drink.

Perhaps a Samaritan woman remembers the same words when a strange young Jew encountered her at Jacob's well and said, "Give me a drink." She had teased him about getting water without a bucket, but he made her a life-changing promise that day.

> Everyone who drinks of this water will be thirsty again, but those who drink of the water that I will give them will never be thirsty. The water that I will give will become in them a spring of water gushing up to eternal life. (John 4:13–14)

Now that spring is dry.

Others may recall when the powerful were watching, following, and plotting against Jesus. One day during the festival of Booths, he stood fearlessly in the middle of Jerusalem and cried aloud:

> Let anyone who is thirsty come to me,
> and let the one who believes in me
> drink. As the scripture has said,
> "Out of the believer's heart shall flow
> rivers of living water." (John 7.37 38)

Now he cries for one single drop.

And then there are the few who need to think back only a few hours to the supper they shared with Jesus. Was this the same person who had handed them the cup of blessing and said:

> Drink from it, all of you; for this is my
> blood of the covenant, which is poured
> out for many, for the forgiveness of
> sins.—Matthew 26:27–28

Now a moistened sponge is his only blessing. Such is the thirst that strikes him on the cross.

OTHER, DEEPER THIRSTS hold Jesus to his cross. Jesus yearns for the coming of God's reign of justice, peace, and joy and to see this world healed of evil.

> How blest are those who hunger
> and thirst to see right prevail;
>   they shall be satisfied.
> (Matthew 5:6, NEB)

Jesus aches with compassion for the hungry, the thirsty, the stranger, the naked ones, the sick, and the prisoners, so much so that he joins them to himself. He once told his followers that when they gave a drink "to one of the least of these who are members of my family, you did it to me" (Matthew 25:40).

Jesus longs to see his beloved Jerusalem repent its rebellion and return to the living God, sheltering once more under God's covenant love. He had lamented before crowds of people, scribes, and Pharisees:

> Jerusalem, Jerusalem, the city that kills the prophets and stones those who are sent to it! How often have I desired to gather your children together as a hen gathers her brood under her wings, but you were not willing! (Matthew 23:37)

These were his deepest thirsts.

Jesus knew that the healing of humanity required winning the battle from within the human condition. Healing could flow only through an entering into and a bearing of suffering and sin. When onlookers sneered, "He saved others; he cannot save himself," they could not see that only because he had *never thought of saving himself* could anybody be saved at all. And those who shouted, "If you are the Son of God, come down from the cross" could not see that it was precisely *because* he was the Son of God that he would not come down from the cross.

In the end, the deepest thirst of this Jesus—the thirst that held him to that cross—was the thirst of unrequited love. Jesus thirsts to see all people discover God's love for them through forgiveness and new life. His dying tells us, *God longs like this, thirsts like this, bleeds like this, always.*

> For God so loved the world, that he gave his only Son. (John 3:16)

No sponge of sour wine can slake that thirst. Only the assurance of our repentance and faith can do that.

For Reflection

Have I allowed the full weight of this word's longing to touch me? When will I recognize God's thirst for my love and respond with my life?

Prayer

Holy Jesus, all the longing of God,
through all the ages, for all humanity,
cries out to me from your cross.
Give me a heart to hear that cry
and a longing to be found by your love.
Amen.

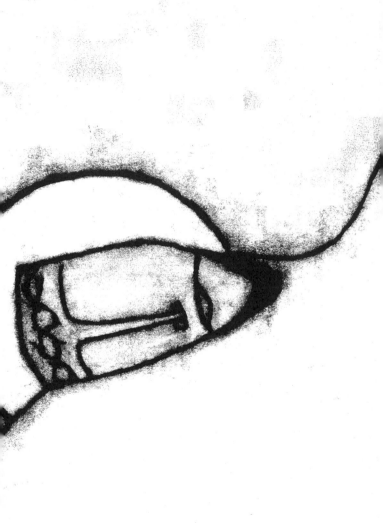

THE SIXTH
AND SEVENTH
WORDS

"It is finished!"

JOHN 19:30

---

*"Father, into your
hands I commend
my spirit."*

LUKE 23:46

❧

When Jesus had received the wine, he said, "It is finished."

—JOHN 19:30

Darkness came over the whole land until three in the afternoon, while the sun's light failed; and the curtain of the temple was torn in two. Then Jesus, crying with a loud voice, said, "Father, into your hands I commend my spirit." Having said this, he breathed his last.

—LUKE 23:44–46

*J*esus has spent six hours on the cross.

It is a strange and bitter irony that the instruments used to bring this agony should be those with which Jesus is most familiar. Wood and nails were once the tools of his trade. The sound of hammer blows was part of his life. He was accustomed to the feel of nails in his hands. He was a shaper of wood—a carpenter.

Every carpenter holds in mind a vision of the finished product, a picture of what the rude timber eventually will become. Through all the work, the wrestling and sweating over stubborn timber, the patience and strength and determination, the shaping and smoothing, that vision remains. At last comes the moment when the carpenter stands back and views the completed work.

It's finished!

None of the furniture Jesus made in his carpenter's shop has survived, but his cross —this wood and these nails—will stand forever as the Carpenter's mightiest work, the work of our salvation. This time, when Jesus heard the hammer blows, he received nails into his own flesh, and another wielded the hammer. But the Carpenter was still at work. He would turn even this wood and these nails into something good and beautiful. His greatest work of all.

In human conflict, a moment often comes when the battle is so finely balanced that each side must commit its last reserves to decide the outcome. There can be no holding back. In the battle between God's love and the gathered forces of evil, Good Friday was that moment.

> O love of God! O sin of man!
>   In this dread act your strength
>   is tried;
>   And victory remains with love:
>   For He, our Lord, is crucified.[1]

Here God did something that changed forever the moral equation of the universe, shifting the balance from evil to good, from the love of power to the power of love.

Now Jesus can say of this, his greatest work, "It is finished!" Now he can go home.

LONG AGO IN the mists of creation, God made a world of goodness and beauty. We are told that God labored to fashion this masterpiece for six days, and when God contemplated the finished work, God smiled. "It was very good" (Genesis 1:31).

And on the seventh day of Creation, God rested.

But then the creatures God made for companionship repudiated their Creator, and the world became an alien place. God's work of loving creation became the rebel planet, made ugly by the hubris of human-kind grasping at being God. That's why Jesus had to come to *reclaim* and *remake* the world.

On Good Friday, in Jesus' breaking heart, the work is completed. Love wrestles to the death with evil and still remains love. Evil is overcome. God's second work of creation is accomplished and, as the seventh hour of Jesus' agony strikes, a seventh and final word is spoken:

> Father, into your hands I commend
> my spirit.

When God sees what the beloved son has done, God weeps. *It is very good.*

And Jesus rests.

Earlier, when we listened to the fourth word of our Lord from the cross, we heard that terrible cry of dereliction, "My God, my God, why have you forsaken me?" The darkness was deep and the loneliness too frightening for words. But the work is done now. Evil's last reserves have been used up. Only love remains. This crucifixion, this drama that changed the world forever, comes to its end with words that once more affirm the intimate trust, the total oneness of Son and Father. "Father, into your hands. . . ." *Take my suffering. Take my sacrifice. Take my spirit.* At last Jesus can rest.

And so can we.

Because of Christ's work on the cross, we too can let go. We can leave the things that hurt, pierce, and suffocate our souls at the foot of the Cross. We can put our faith in the one who has spoken these seven great words and invite him to re-create us, to reshape our lives through his passion. Christ has changed the lives of so many.

My father was one such person. Even as a child, I saw a goodness, an integrity, and a beauty in his character that I instinctively knew was not of his own making. After he died, I found this scrap of verse among his papers, and it said everything.

O Master Carpenter of Nazareth,
Who at the last, with wood and nails

Purchased our whole salvation,
Wield well thy tools in this,
   thy workshop,
That we who come to thy bench
   rough–hewn,
May be fashioned to a truer beauty by
   thy hand.[2]

We can say to this Master Carpenter, "Jesus, into your hands I commit my spirit," and we will receive the promise of something new. He will fashion us into a more true and more beautiful soul.

Bible scholar Hans–Reudi Weber once taught me something I had never noticed about the Passion story.[3] Like so many people, I had always linked the darkness that covered the land with the death of Jesus. It is not so. The darkness descends over Jesus' *suffering* on Calvary from noon until three o'clock—until the moment Jesus bows his head and dies. Then it lifts! The moment Jesus dies, the darkness is gone!

Easter is yet to be, but its promise has begun to dawn.

⌐∼◡

FOR REFLECTION

To what burden in my life are these words speaking? To what place of struggle do they declare closure and invite trusting rest? How completely have I committed my life—body, mind, and spirit—to this God, this Savior?

Prayer

Rest now, Holy Jesus, hero of the Cross.
Your work is done.
The world has done its sinning, and
you have done your loving,
each beyond limit.
And, at the end, limitless love prevails.
Your dying becomes my hope and the
hope of the world.
Amen.

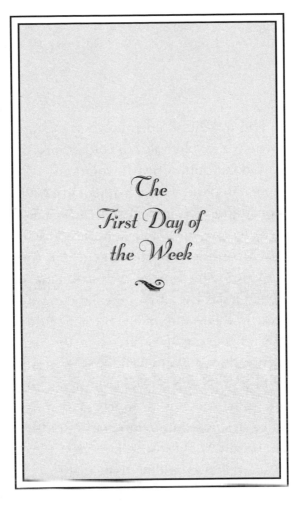

The
First Day of
the Week

About a hundred miles east of Cape Town, where I live, lies the oldest mission station in South Africa. It was founded by Moravian pastor Georg Schmidt in 1738 in a beautiful wooded valley that he called Genadendal—the "Valley of Grace." To this day, according to Moravian custom, very early on Easter Sunday, the inhabitants of Genadendal rise quietly in the darkness, pick up their equipment, and make their way to the cemetery. There in the dark silence, they wait, until suddenly . . . as the first rays of dawn break the horizon, they put trombones and trumpets to their lips, and a Resurrection hymn crashes out triumphantly among the tombstones: "Christ the Lord is risen today! Hallelujah!"

Christians are the only people who can sing hallelujahs in a graveyard, all because of what happened on that "first day of the week," long ago.

⁓

THE WOMEN WHO had watched longest on Friday were also up earliest on the first day of the week. In the gloomy mists of the morning, before the sun had risen, they made their way to the garden tomb. Since sunset on Friday, the scarred and broken body had been locked into this cold, dark place of the dead. Now it was Sunday, and the women were here to do what they'd had no time to do on Sabbath-eve: to wash and anoint the body properly. They came to complete the burial of a corpse. Instead, they found the tomb wide open, the body gone, and the only occupant someone who asked them why they were looking for the living among the dead.

Sometime during the night, life had been breathed into the corpse; the stone had been rolled away; Jesus had gone out of the cave of death into the garden of the morning.

By a mighty act of Resurrection, the Father, into whose hands Jesus had committed his spirit, honors for all time the Son's self–giving. God names Jesus' cross of shame, where sin and death did their worst but were overwhelmed by total love, as our place of salvation. Resurrection is God's resounding "Yes!" to the word of saving love and identification spoken from that cross.

> When sin had flung its last dart and said its last word, He answered them from His Cross. If we may dare to say so, He there betrothed himself for ever to the human race, for better, for worse, for richer, for poorer, in sickness and in health. Seven words from the Cross are

reported, but there was another, which said: "I will never leave you nor forsake you." It was said by the only begotten Son of God with full purpose of heart, and it has never been unsaid. That pledge stands for ever. . . . It binds Him: it confronts us. Every one of us must reckon with that word—or, rather, with the One who said the word.[1]

It's true: Christ will never leave us or forsake us. Because death could not hold him, life can never exclude him now. Therefore a living Christ still confronts us with the words of the dying Jesus. When we make space for those words to speak into our souls, we are changed forever.

Prayer

Holy Jesus, I hear God's mighty "Yes!" in
    your Resurrection
You invite me to live also,
and I want to say "Yes!" to you.

Take me out of the tomb that
        imprisons me,
lead me into the morning of new life,
and walk with me wherever your love
        may lead.
Amen.

Notes

THE SECOND WORD

1. George Bernard Shaw in a press interview in early 1948. Information kindly supplied by Dianne S. Uttley, the Bernard Shaw Information and Research Service, London, England.

2. In a PBS program entitled *Archbishop Desmond Tutu with Bill Moyers*, released in 1999.

THE SIXTH AND SEVENTH WORDS

1. Frederick William Faber, *The Methodist Hymn-Book* (London: Methodist Conference Office, 1933), no. 187.

2. Author unknown. I found this "Carpenter's Prayer" among my father's papers. It has always been precious to me.

3. Hans-Reudi Weber, then on the staff of the World Council of Churches, made

this observation in discussion following one of the Bible studies he conducted, and which I attended, at the South African Congress on Mission and Evangelism, Durban, 1973.

THE FIRST DAY OF THE WEEK

1. W. Russell Maltby, *Christ and His Cross*, 2nd ed. (London: The Epworth Press, 1936), 94–95.

ABOUT THE AUTHOR

PETER STOREY has been in active ministry for four decades. Currently he is Ruth W. and A. Morris Williams Professor of the Practice of Christian Ministry at Duke Divinity School. He is a former bishop of the Johannesburg/Soweto area and national leader of the Methodist Church of Southern Africa. In these positions and as president of the South African Council of Churches, working closely with Arch bishop Desmond Tutu, he helped give leadership to the church's antiapartheid struggle. He has played key roles in peace-making structures in South Africa and was appointed by President Nelson Mandela to help select the nation's Truth and Reconciliation Commission. His first love is preaching the gospel.

About the Artist

Jan L. Richardson, an ordained minister in the Florida Conference of The United Methodist Church, currently serves as visiting artist at First United Methodist Church of Winter Park, Florida. She is also a retreat and workshop leader, spiritual director, and author. Her books include *Sacred Journeys: A Woman's Book of Daily Prayer*; *Night Visions: Searching the Shadows of Advent and Christmas*; and *In Wisdom's Path: Discovering the Sacred in Every Season*. Jan is a faculty member of the Grünewald Guild in Leavenworth, Washington; a contributing editor for *The Other Side* magazine; and an oblate novice of Saint Brigid of Kildare Monastery, a Methodist–Benedictine community in Saint Joseph, Minnesota.

MORE RESOURCES
FROM
UPPER ROOM BOOKS

From the Edge of the Crowd: Meditations for Lent by James E. Sargent ISBN 0-8358-9854-7

Forward to Freedom: From Exodus to Easter by David Adam ISBN 0-8358-0944-7

The Rising: Living the Mysteries of Lent, Easter, and Pentecost by Wendy M. Wright ISBN 0-8358-0716-9

Traveling the Prayer Paths of Jesus by John Indermark ISBN 0-8358 9857 1

Wilderness Wanderings: A Lenten Pilgrimage by Marilyn Brown Oden ISBN 0-8358-0743-6

Available from your local bookseller
or call 1-800-972-0433
or order online at
www.upperroom.org